LIFE
ULTIMATE PLANNER

October - December 2023

Q4

THIS PLANNER BELONGS TO

_____
NAME

_____
EMAIL

_____
CELL

GET STARTED

The Life Ultimate Planner is designed for anyone who wants to make their life count for more. It is a tool, a road map to be successful. The Life Ultimate Planner will help you create alignment with your life priorities. You will have increased confidence with decision making. You will find yourself in the drivers seat of life, feel organized and respected as an inspirational leader. It is the planner designed for people who love to plan, as well as those who need help planning. Start slow, set your own pace, but commit to it and watch your life become more manageable and productive.

Copyright©2023 Cheryl Jackson. All rights reserved.

ISBN: 978-1-960130-06-8

www.LiveLifeFullyCoaching.com

CONTENTS

2023 Calendar 4
2024 Calendar 5

October 2023 Calendar 6
October Master Success Actions 8
October Weekly and Daily Pages 10
October Income Tracker 60
October Expense Tracker 61
October Savings Tracker 62
October Monthly Progress 63

November 2023 Calendar 64
November Master Success Actions 66
November Weekly and Daily Pages 68
November Income Tracker 108
November Expense Tracker 109
November Savings Tracker 110
November Monthly Progress 111

December 2023 Calendar 112
December Master Success Actions 114
December Weekly and Daily Pages 116
December Income Tracker 156
December Expense Tracker 158
December Savings Tracker 158
December Monthly Progress 159

Books to Read 160
Wish List 161
Notes Pages 162
Index 182

2023 CALENDAR

JANUARY

M	T	W	T	F	S	S
						1
2	3	4	5	6	7	8
9	10	11	12	13	14	15
16	17	18	19	20	21	22
23	24	25	26	27	28	29
30	31					

FEBRUARY

M	T	W	T	F	S	S
		1	2	3	4	5
6	7	8	9	10	11	12
13	14	15	16	17	18	19
20	21	22	23	24	25	26
27	28					

MARCH

M	T	W	T	F	S	S
		1	2	3	4	5
6	7	8	9	10	11	12
13	14	15	16	17	18	19
20	21	22	23	24	25	26
27	28	29	30	31		

APRIL

M	T	W	T	F	S	S
					1	2
3	4	5	6	7	8	9
10	11	12	13	14	15	16
17	18	19	20	21	22	23
24	25	26	27	28	29	30

MAY

M	T	W	T	F	S	S
1	2	3	4	5	6	7
8	9	10	11	12	13	14
15	16	17	18	19	20	21
22	23	24	25	26	27	28
29	30	31				

JUNE

M	T	W	T	F	S	S
			1	2	3	4
5	6	7	8	9	10	11
12	13	14	15	16	17	18
19	20	21	22	23	24	25
26	27	28	29	30		

JULY

M	T	W	T	F	S	S
					1	2
3	4	5	6	7	8	9
10	11	12	13	14	15	16
17	18	19	20	21	22	23
24	25	26	27	28	29	30
31						

AUGUST

M	T	W	T	F	S	S
	1	2	3	4	5	6
7	8	9	10	11	12	13
14	15	16	17	18	19	20
21	22	23	24	25	26	27
28	29	30	31			

SEPTEMBER

M	T	W	T	F	S	S
				1	2	3
4	5	6	7	8	9	10
11	12	13	14	15	16	17
18	19	20	21	22	23	24
25	26	27	28	29	30	

OCTOBER

M	T	W	T	F	S	S
						1
2	3	4	5	6	7	8
9	10	11	12	13	14	15
16	17	18	19	20	21	22
23	24	25	26	27	28	29
30	31					

NOVEMBER

M	T	W	T	F	S	S
		1	2	3	4	5
6	7	8	9	10	11	12
13	14	15	16	17	18	19
20	21	22	23	24	25	26
27	28	29	30			

DECEMBER

M	T	W	T	F	S	S
				1	2	3
4	5	6	7	8	9	10
11	12	13	14	15	16	17
18	19	20	21	22	23	24
25	26	27	28	29	30	31

2024 CALENDAR

JANUARY
M	T	W	T	F	S	S
1	2	3	4	5	6	7
8	9	10	11	12	13	14
15	16	17	18	19	20	21
22	23	24	25	26	27	28
29	30	31				

FEBRUARY
M	T	W	T	F	S	S
			1	2	3	4
5	6	7	8	9	10	11
12	13	14	15	16	17	18
19	20	21	22	23	24	25
26	27	28	29			

MARCH
M	T	W	T	F	S	S
				1	2	3
4	5	6	7	8	9	10
11	12	13	14	15	16	17
18	19	20	21	22	23	24
25	26	27	28	29	30	31

APRIL
M	T	W	T	F	S	S
1	2	3	4	5	6	7
8	9	10	11	12	13	14
15	16	17	18	19	20	21
22	23	24	25	26	27	28
29	30					

MAY
M	T	W	T	F	S	S
		1	2	3	4	5
6	7	8	9	10	11	12
13	14	15	16	17	18	19
20	21	22	23	24	25	26
27	28	29	30	31		

JUNE
M	T	W	T	F	S	S
					1	2
3	4	5	6	7	8	9
10	11	12	13	14	15	16
17	18	19	20	21	22	23
24	25	26	27	28	29	30

JULY
M	T	W	T	F	S	S
1	2	3	4	5	6	7
8	9	10	11	12	13	14
15	16	17	18	19	20	21
22	23	24	25	26	27	28
29	30	31				

AUGUST
M	T	W	T	F	S	S
			1	2	3	4
5	6	7	8	9	10	11
12	13	14	15	16	17	18
19	20	21	22	23	24	25
26	27	28	29	30	31	

SEPTEMBER
M	T	W	T	F	S	S
						1
2	3	4	5	6	7	8
9	10	11	12	13	14	15
16	17	18	19	20	21	22
23	24	25	26	27	28	29
30						

OCTOBER
M	T	W	T	F	S	S
	1	2	3	4	5	6
7	8	9	10	11	12	13
14	15	16	17	18	19	20
21	22	23	24	25	26	27
28	29	30	31			

NOVEMBER
M	T	W	T	F	S	S
				1	2	3
4	5	6	7	8	9	10
11	12	13	14	15	16	17
18	19	20	21	22	23	24
25	26	27	28	29	30	

DECEMBER
M	T	W	T	F	S	S
						1
2	3	4	5	6	7	8
9	10	11	12	13	14	15
16	17	18	19	20	21	22
23	24	25	26	27	28	29
30	31					

OCTOBER

MONDAY	TUESDAY	WEDNESDAY	THURSDAY
2	3	4	5
9	10	11	12
16	17	18	19
23	24	25	26
30	31		

GOALS

2023

FRIDAY	SATURDAY	SUNDAY	NOTES
6	7	8	
13	14	15	
20	21	22	
24	28	29	

NOTES

MASTER SUCCESS ACTIONS
OCTOBER 2023

List 4 life areas and your goals to focus on this month:

1.

2.

3.

4.

Use this master task list for the big action steps you will commit to do this month. They will accomplish the goals you set to improve your life in the 4 areas of focus. Your daily tasks will be the small steps to accomplish these bigger steps.

DONE	SUCCESS ACTIONS

NOTES

WEEKLY PLANNER

QUOTE OF THE WEEK:

MONDAY 2
TUESDAY 3
WEDNESDAY 4
THURSDAY 5
FRIDAY 6
SATURDAY 7
SUNDAY 8

SUCCESS FOCUS:

PRIORITIES / GOALS

○
○
○
○
○
○
○
○
○
○

NOTES

OCTOBER 2 – 8, 2023

	BREAKFAST	LUNCH	DINNER	SNACKS
M				
T				
W				
T				
F				
S				
S				

SHOPPING LIST:

NOTES

MONDAY
OCTOBER 2023

2

TODAY'S PRAYER & FOCUS:

SCHEDULE

TIME	APPOINTMENT

PRIORITIES / GOALS

○
○
○
○
○
○
○
○
○
○

NOTES & SCRIBBLES

HABITS – 1 NEW PER MONTH

1.
2.
3.

TODAY I'M GRATEFUL FOR

3

TUESDAY
OCTOBER 2023

TODAY'S PRAYER & FOCUS:

SCHEDULE

TIME	APPOINTMENT

PRIORITIES / GOALS

- ○
- ○
- ○
- ○
- ○
- ○
- ○
- ○
- ○
- ○

NOTES & SCRIBBLES

HABITS – 1 NEW PER MONTH

1.
2.
3.

TODAY I'M GRATEFUL FOR

WEDNESDAY
OCTOBER 2023

4

TODAY'S PRAYER & FOCUS:

SCHEDULE

TIME	APPOINTMENT

PRIORITIES / GOALS

- ◯
- ◯
- ◯
- ◯
- ◯
- ◯
- ◯
- ◯
- ◯
- ◯

NOTES & SCRIBBLES

HABITS – 1 NEW PER MONTH

1.
2.
3.

TODAY I'M GRATEFUL FOR

5

THURSDAY
OCTOBER 2023

TODAY'S PRAYER & FOCUS:

SCHEDULE

TIME	APPOINTMENT

PRIORITIES / GOALS

- ○
- ○
- ○
- ○
- ○
- ○
- ○
- ○
- ○
- ○

NOTES & SCRIBBLES

HABITS — 1 NEW PER MONTH

1.
2.
3.

TODAY I'M GRATEFUL FOR

FRIDAY
OCTOBER 2023
6

TODAY'S PRAYER & FOCUS:

SCHEDULE

TIME	APPOINTMENT

PRIORITIES / GOALS

- ○
- ○
- ○
- ○
- ○
- ○
- ○
- ○
- ○
- ○

NOTES & SCRIBBLES

HABITS – 1 NEW PER MONTH
1.
2.
3.

TODAY I'M GRATEFUL FOR

7

SATURDAY
OCTOBER 2023

TODAY'S PRAYER & FOCUS:

SCHEDULE

TIME	APPOINTMENT

PRIORITIES / GOALS

- ○
- ○
- ○
- ○
- ○
- ○
- ○
- ○
- ○
- ○

NOTES & SCRIBBLES

HABITS – 1 NEW PER MONTH

1.
2.
3.

TODAY I'M GRATEFUL FOR

SUNDAY
OCTOBER 2023

8

TODAY'S PRAYER & FOCUS:

SCHEDULE

TIME	APPOINTMENT

PRIORITIES / GOALS

- ◯
- ◯
- ◯
- ◯
- ◯
- ◯
- ◯
- ◯
- ◯
- ◯

NOTES & SCRIBBLES

HABITS – 1 NEW PER MONTH

1.
2.
3.

TODAY I'M GRATEFUL FOR

WEEKLY PLANNER

QUOTE OF THE WEEK:

MONDAY 9	**PRIORITIES / GOALS**
TUESDAY 10	○
	○
WEDNESDAY 11	○
	○
THURSDAY 12	○
	○
FRIDAY 13	○
SATURDAY 14	**NOTES**
SUNDAY 15	

SUCCESS FOCUS:

OCTOBER 9 – 15, 2023

	BREAKFAST	LUNCH	DINNER	SNACKS
M				
T				
W				
T				
F				
S				
S				

SHOPPING LIST:

NOTES

MONDAY
OCTOBER 2023
9

TODAY'S PRAYER & FOCUS:

SCHEDULE

TIME	APPOINTMENT

PRIORITIES / GOALS

- ◯
- ◯
- ◯
- ◯
- ◯
- ◯
- ◯
- ◯
- ◯
- ◯

NOTES & SCRIBBLES

HABITS – 1 NEW PER MONTH

1.
2.
3.

TODAY I'M GRATEFUL FOR

10

TUESDAY
OCTOBER 2023

TODAY'S PRAYER & FOCUS:

SCHEDULE

TIME	APPOINTMENT

PRIORITIES / GOALS

- ◯
- ◯
- ◯
- ◯
- ◯
- ◯
- ◯
- ◯
- ◯
- ◯

NOTES & SCRIBBLES

HABITS — 1 NEW PER MONTH

1.
2.
3.

TODAY I'M GRATEFUL FOR

WEDNESDAY
OCTOBER 2023

11

TODAY'S PRAYER & FOCUS:

SCHEDULE

TIME	APPOINTMENT

PRIORITIES / GOALS

- ○
- ○
- ○
- ○
- ○
- ○
- ○
- ○
- ○
- ○

NOTES & SCRIBBLES

HABITS — 1 NEW PER MONTH

1.
2.
3.

TODAY I'M GRATEFUL FOR

12
THURSDAY
OCTOBER 2023

TODAY'S PRAYER & FOCUS:

SCHEDULE

TIME	APPOINTMENT

PRIORITIES / GOALS

- ◯
- ◯
- ◯
- ◯
- ◯
- ◯
- ◯
- ◯
- ◯
- ◯

NOTES & SCRIBBLES

HABITS — 1 NEW PER MONTH

1.
2.
3.

TODAY I'M GRATEFUL FOR

FRIDAY
OCTOBER 2023
13

TODAY'S PRAYER & FOCUS:

SCHEDULE

TIME	APPOINTMENT

PRIORITIES / GOALS

- ○
- ○
- ○
- ○
- ○
- ○
- ○
- ○
- ○
- ○

NOTES & SCRIBBLES

HABITS – 1 NEW PER MONTH

1.
2.
3.

TODAY I'M GRATEFUL FOR

14

SATURDAY
OCTOBER 2023

TODAY'S PRAYER & FOCUS:

SCHEDULE

TIME	APPOINTMENT

PRIORITIES / GOALS

- ○
- ○
- ○
- ○
- ○
- ○
- ○
- ○
- ○
- ○

NOTES & SCRIBBLES

HABITS – 1 NEW PER MONTH

1.
2.
3.

TODAY I'M GRATEFUL FOR

SUNDAY
OCTOBER 2023 **15**

TODAY'S PRAYER & FOCUS:

SCHEDULE

TIME	APPOINTMENT

PRIORITIES / GOALS

- ○
- ○
- ○
- ○
- ○
- ○
- ○
- ○
- ○
- ○

NOTES & SCRIBBLES

HABITS – 1 NEW PER MONTH

1.
2.
3.

TODAY I'M GRATEFUL FOR

WEEKLY PLANNER

QUOTE OF THE WEEK:

MONDAY 16
TUESDAY 17
WEDNESDAY 18
THURSDAY 19
FRIDAY 20
SATURDAY 21
SUNDAY 22

SUCCESS FOCUS:

PRIORITIES / GOALS

- ◯
- ◯
- ◯
- ◯
- ◯
- ◯
- ◯
- ◯
- ◯

NOTES

OCTOBER 16 – 22, 2023

	BREAKFAST	LUNCH	DINNER	SNACKS
M				
T				
W				
T				
F				
S				
S				

SHOPPING LIST:

NOTES

MONDAY
OCTOBER 2023 **16**

TODAY'S PRAYER & FOCUS:

SCHEDULE

TIME	APPOINTMENT

PRIORITIES / GOALS

- ○
- ○
- ○
- ○
- ○
- ○
- ○
- ○
- ○
- ○

NOTES & SCRIBBLES

HABITS – 1 NEW PER MONTH

1.
2.
3.

TODAY I'M GRATEFUL FOR

17

TUESDAY
OCTOBER 2023

TODAY'S PRAYER & FOCUS:

SCHEDULE

TIME	APPOINTMENT

PRIORITIES / GOALS

- ○
- ○
- ○
- ○
- ○
- ○
- ○
- ○
- ○
- ○

NOTES & SCRIBBLES

HABITS – 1 NEW PER MONTH

1.
2.
3.

TODAY I'M GRATEFUL FOR

WEDNESDAY
OCTOBER 2023
18

TODAY'S PRAYER & FOCUS:

SCHEDULE

TIME	APPOINTMENT

PRIORITIES / GOALS

- ○
- ○
- ○
- ○
- ○
- ○
- ○
- ○
- ○
- ○

NOTES & SCRIBBLES

HABITS – 1 NEW PER MONTH

1.
2.
3.

TODAY I'M GRATEFUL FOR

19

THURSDAY
OCTOBER 2023

TODAY'S PRAYER & FOCUS:

SCHEDULE

TIME	APPOINTMENT

PRIORITIES / GOALS

- ○
- ○
- ○
- ○
- ○
- ○
- ○
- ○
- ○
- ○

NOTES & SCRIBBLES

HABITS – 1 NEW PER MONTH

1.
2.
3.

TODAY I'M GRATEFUL FOR

FRIDAY
OCTOBER 2023 **20**

TODAY'S PRAYER & FOCUS:

SCHEDULE

TIME	APPOINTMENT

PRIORITIES / GOALS

- ○
- ○
- ○
- ○
- ○
- ○
- ○
- ○
- ○
- ○

NOTES & SCRIBBLES

HABITS – 1 NEW PER MONTH

1.
2.
3.

TODAY I'M GRATEFUL FOR

21

SATURDAY
OCTOBER 2023

TODAY'S PRAYER & FOCUS:

SCHEDULE

TIME	APPOINTMENT

PRIORITIES / GOALS

- ○
- ○
- ○
- ○
- ○
- ○
- ○
- ○
- ○
- ○

NOTES & SCRIBBLES

HABITS – 1 NEW PER MONTH

1.
2.
3.

TODAY I'M GRATEFUL FOR

SUNDAY
OCTOBER 2023
22

TODAY'S PRAYER & FOCUS:

SCHEDULE

TIME	APPOINTMENT

PRIORITIES / GOALS

- ◯
- ◯
- ◯
- ◯
- ◯
- ◯
- ◯
- ◯
- ◯
- ◯

NOTES & SCRIBBLES

HABITS – 1 NEW PER MONTH

1.
2.
3.

TODAY I'M GRATEFUL FOR

WEEKLY PLANNER

QUOTE OF THE WEEK:

| MONDAY |
| 23 |

| TUESDAY |
| 24 |

| WEDNESDAY |
| 25 |

| THURSDAY |
| 26 |

| FRIDAY |
| 27 |

| SATURDAY |
| 28 |

| SUNDAY |
| 29 |

SUCCESS FOCUS:

PRIORITIES / GOALS

○
○
○
○
○
○
○
○
○

NOTES

OCTOBER 23 – 29, 2023

	BREAKFAST	LUNCH	DINNER	SNACKS
M				
T				
W				
T				
F				
S				
S				

SHOPPING LIST:

NOTES

MONDAY
OCTOBER 2023
23

TODAY'S PRAYER & FOCUS:

SCHEDULE

TIME	APPOINTMENT

PRIORITIES / GOALS

- ○
- ○
- ○
- ○
- ○
- ○
- ○
- ○
- ○
- ○

NOTES & SCRIBBLES

HABITS – 1 NEW PER MONTH

1.
2.
3.

TODAY I'M GRATEFUL FOR

24

TUESDAY
OCTOBER 2023

TODAY'S PRAYER & FOCUS:

SCHEDULE

TIME	APPOINTMENT

PRIORITIES / GOALS

- ◯
- ◯
- ◯
- ◯
- ◯
- ◯
- ◯
- ◯
- ◯
- ◯

NOTES & SCRIBBLES

HABITS – 1 NEW PER MONTH

1.
2.
3.

TODAY I'M GRATEFUL FOR

**WEDNESDAY
OCTOBER 2023**

25

TODAY'S PRAYER & FOCUS:

SCHEDULE

TIME	APPOINTMENT

PRIORITIES / GOALS

- ◯
- ◯
- ◯
- ◯
- ◯
- ◯
- ◯
- ◯
- ◯
- ◯

NOTES & SCRIBBLES

HABITS – 1 NEW PER MONTH

1.
2.
3.

TODAY I'M GRATEFUL FOR

26

THURSDAY
OCTOBER 2023

TODAY'S PRAYER & FOCUS:

SCHEDULE

TIME	APPOINTMENT

PRIORITIES / GOALS

- ○
- ○
- ○
- ○
- ○
- ○
- ○
- ○
- ○
- ○

NOTES & SCRIBBLES

HABITS – 1 NEW PER MONTH

1.
2.
3.

TODAY I'M GRATEFUL FOR

FRIDAY
OCTOBER 2023 **27**

TODAY'S PRAYER & FOCUS:

SCHEDULE

TIME	APPOINTMENT

PRIORITIES / GOALS

- ○
- ○
- ○
- ○
- ○
- ○
- ○
- ○
- ○
- ○

NOTES & SCRIBBLES

HABITS – 1 NEW PER MONTH

1.
2.
3.

TODAY I'M GRATEFUL FOR

28
SATURDAY
OCTOBER 2023

TODAY'S PRAYER & FOCUS:

SCHEDULE

TIME	APPOINTMENT

PRIORITIES / GOALS

- ◯
- ◯
- ◯
- ◯
- ◯
- ◯
- ◯
- ◯
- ◯
- ◯

NOTES & SCRIBBLES

HABITS – 1 NEW PER MONTH

1.
2.
3.

TODAY I'M GRATEFUL FOR

SUNDAY
OCTOBER 2023
29

TODAY'S PRAYER & FOCUS:

SCHEDULE

TIME	APPOINTMENT

PRIORITIES / GOALS

- ○
- ○
- ○
- ○
- ○
- ○
- ○
- ○
- ○
- ○

NOTES & SCRIBBLES

HABITS – 1 NEW PER MONTH

1.
2.
3.

TODAY I'M GRATEFUL FOR

WEEKLY PLANNER

QUOTE OF THE WEEK:

MONDAY 30

TUESDAY 31

WEDNESDAY 1

THURSDAY 2

FRIDAY 3

SATURDAY 4

SUNDAY 5

SUCCESS FOCUS:

PRIORITIES / GOALS

- ○
- ○
- ○
- ○
- ○
- ○
- ○
- ○
- ○

NOTES

OCTOBER 30 – NOVEMBER 5, 2023

	BREAKFAST	LUNCH	DINNER	SNACKS
M				
T				
W				
T				
F				
S				
S				

SHOPPING LIST:

NOTES

MONDAY
OCTOBER 2023
30

TODAY'S PRAYER & FOCUS:

SCHEDULE

TIME	APPOINTMENT

PRIORITIES / GOALS

- ○
- ○
- ○
- ○
- ○
- ○
- ○
- ○
- ○
- ○

NOTES & SCRIBBLES

HABITS – 1 NEW PER MONTH

1.
2.
3.

TODAY I'M GRATEFUL FOR

31

TUESDAY
OCTOBER 2023

TODAY'S PRAYER & FOCUS:

SCHEDULE

TIME	APPOINTMENT

PRIORITIES / GOALS

- ○
- ○
- ○
- ○
- ○
- ○
- ○
- ○
- ○
- ○

NOTES & SCRIBBLES

HABITS – 1 NEW PER MONTH

1.
2.
3.

TODAY I'M GRATEFUL FOR

WEDNESDAY
NOVEMBER 2023

1

TODAY'S PRAYER & FOCUS:

SCHEDULE

TIME	APPOINTMENT

PRIORITIES / GOALS

- ○
- ○
- ○
- ○
- ○
- ○
- ○
- ○
- ○
- ○

NOTES & SCRIBBLES

HABITS – 1 NEW PER MONTH
1.
2.
3.

TODAY I'M GRATEFUL FOR

2

THURSDAY
NOVEMBER 2023

TODAY'S PRAYER & FOCUS:

SCHEDULE

TIME	APPOINTMENT

PRIORITIES / GOALS

- ◯
- ◯
- ◯
- ◯
- ◯
- ◯
- ◯
- ◯
- ◯
- ◯

NOTES & SCRIBBLES

HABITS – 1 NEW PER MONTH

1.
2.
3.

TODAY I'M GRATEFUL FOR

FRIDAY
NOVEMBER 2023

3

TODAY'S PRAYER & FOCUS:

SCHEDULE

TIME	APPOINTMENT

PRIORITIES / GOALS

- ○
- ○
- ○
- ○
- ○
- ○
- ○
- ○
- ○
- ○

NOTES & SCRIBBLES

HABITS – 1 NEW PER MONTH

1.
2.
3.

TODAY I'M GRATEFUL FOR

4

SATURDAY
NOVEMBER 2023

TODAY'S PRAYER & FOCUS:

SCHEDULE

TIME	APPOINTMENT

PRIORITIES / GOALS

- ○
- ○
- ○
- ○
- ○
- ○
- ○
- ○
- ○
- ○

NOTES & SCRIBBLES

HABITS – 1 NEW PER MONTH

1.
2.
3.

TODAY I'M GRATEFUL FOR

SUNDAY
NOVEMBER 2023

5

TODAY'S PRAYER & FOCUS:

SCHEDULE

TIME	APPOINTMENT

PRIORITIES / GOALS

- ○
- ○
- ○
- ○
- ○
- ○
- ○
- ○
- ○
- ○

NOTES & SCRIBBLES

HABITS – 1 NEW PER MONTH

1.
2.
3.

TODAY I'M GRATEFUL FOR

OCTOBER 2023 INCOME TRACKER

DATE	INCOME	CATEGORY	AMOUNT
TOTAL			

OCTOBER 2023 EXPENSE TRACKER

DATE	EXPENSE	CATEGORY	AMOUNT
TOTAL			

OCTOBER 2023 SAVINGS TRACKER

SAVING FOR: _____   GOAL AMOUNT: _____

DATE	NOTES	AMOUNT	BALANCE
TOTAL			

MONTHLY PROGRESS - OCTOBER 2023

I HAVE ACHIEVED...

I AM THANKFUL...

I'D LIKE TO IMPROVE...

HOW I WILL CELEBRATE WHAT I DID WELL...

NOVEMBER

MONDAY	TUESDAY	WEDNESDAY	THURSDAY
		1	2
6	7	8	9
13	14	15	16
20	21	22	23
27	28	29	30

GOALS

2023

FRIDAY	SATURDAY	SUNDAY	NOTES
3	4	5	
10	11	12	
17	18	19	
24	25	26	

NOTES

MASTER SUCCESS ACTIONS
NOVEMBER 2023

List 4 life areas and your goals to focus on this month:

1.

2.

3.

4.

Use this master task list for the big action steps you will commit to do this month. They will accomplish the goals you set to improve your life in the 4 areas of focus. Your daily tasks will be the small steps to accomplish these bigger steps.

DONE	SUCCESS ACTIONS

NOTES

WEEKLY PLANNER

QUOTE OF THE WEEK:

MONDAY
6

TUESDAY
7

WEDNESDAY
8

THURSDAY
9

FRIDAY
10

SATURDAY
11

SUNDAY
12

SUCCESS FOCUS:

PRIORITIES / GOALS

-
-
-
-
-
-
-
-
-
-

NOTES

NOVEMBER 6 – 12, 2023

	BREAKFAST	LUNCH	DINNER	SNACKS
M				
T				
W				
T				
F				
S				
S				

SHOPPING LIST:

NOTES

MONDAY
NOVEMBER 2023
6

TODAY'S PRAYER & FOCUS:

SCHEDULE

TIME	APPOINTMENT

PRIORITIES / GOALS

- ○
- ○
- ○
- ○
- ○
- ○
- ○
- ○
- ○
- ○

NOTES & SCRIBBLES

HABITS — 1 NEW PER MONTH

1.
2.
3.

TODAY I'M GRATEFUL FOR

7

TUESDAY
NOVEMBER 2023

TODAY'S PRAYER & FOCUS:

SCHEDULE

TIME	APPOINTMENT

PRIORITIES / GOALS

- ○
- ○
- ○
- ○
- ○
- ○
- ○
- ○
- ○
- ○

NOTES & SCRIBBLES

HABITS – 1 NEW PER MONTH

1.
2.
3.

TODAY I'M GRATEFUL FOR

WEDNESDAY
NOVEMBER 2023

8

TODAY'S PRAYER & FOCUS:

SCHEDULE

TIME	APPOINTMENT

PRIORITIES / GOALS

- ○
- ○
- ○
- ○
- ○
- ○
- ○
- ○
- ○
- ○

NOTES & SCRIBBLES

HABITS – 1 NEW PER MONTH

1.
2.
3.

TODAY I'M GRATEFUL FOR

9

THURSDAY
NOVEMBER 2023

TODAY'S PRAYER & FOCUS:

SCHEDULE

TIME	APPOINTMENT

PRIORITIES / GOALS

- ◯
- ◯
- ◯
- ◯
- ◯
- ◯
- ◯
- ◯
- ◯
- ◯

NOTES & SCRIBBLES

HABITS – 1 NEW PER MONTH

1.
2.
3.

TODAY I'M GRATEFUL FOR

FRIDAY
NOVEMBER 2023
10

TODAY'S PRAYER & FOCUS:

SCHEDULE

TIME	APPOINTMENT

PRIORITIES / GOALS

- ○
- ○
- ○
- ○
- ○
- ○
- ○
- ○
- ○
- ○

NOTES & SCRIBBLES

HABITS – 1 NEW PER MONTH

1.
2.
3.

TODAY I'M GRATEFUL FOR

11

SATURDAY
NOVEMBER 2023

TODAY'S PRAYER & FOCUS:

SCHEDULE

TIME	APPOINTMENT

PRIORITIES / GOALS

○
○
○
○
○
○
○
○
○
○

NOTES & SCRIBBLES

HABITS – 1 NEW PER MONTH

1.
2.
3.

TODAY I'M GRATEFUL FOR

SUNDAY
NOVEMBER 2023 **12**

TODAY'S PRAYER & FOCUS:

SCHEDULE

TIME	APPOINTMENT

PRIORITIES / GOALS

- ◯
- ◯
- ◯
- ◯
- ◯
- ◯
- ◯
- ◯
- ◯
- ◯

NOTES & SCRIBBLES

HABITS – 1 NEW PER MONTH

1.
2.
3.

TODAY I'M GRATEFUL FOR

WEEKLY PLANNER

QUOTE OF THE WEEK:

MONDAY 13	**PRIORITIES / GOALS**
TUESDAY 14	○ _____ ○ _____ ○ _____ ○ _____
WEDNESDAY 15	○ _____ ○ _____
THURSDAY 16	○ _____ ○ _____ ○ _____
FRIDAY 17	○ _____
SATURDAY 18	**NOTES**
SUNDAY 19	
SUCCESS FOCUS:	

NOVEMBER 13 – 19, 2023

	BREAKFAST	LUNCH	DINNER	SNACKS
M				
T				
W				
T				
F				
S				
S				

SHOPPING LIST:

NOTES

MONDAY
NOVEMBER 2023
13

TODAY'S PRAYER & FOCUS:

SCHEDULE

TIME	APPOINTMENT

PRIORITIES / GOALS

- ○
- ○
- ○
- ○
- ○
- ○
- ○
- ○
- ○
- ○

NOTES & SCRIBBLES

HABITS – 1 NEW PER MONTH

1.
2.
3.

TODAY I'M GRATEFUL FOR

14

TUESDAY
NOVEMBER 2023

TODAY'S PRAYER & FOCUS:

SCHEDULE

TIME	APPOINTMENT

PRIORITIES / GOALS

- ○
- ○
- ○
- ○
- ○
- ○
- ○
- ○
- ○
- ○

NOTES & SCRIBBLES

HABITS – 1 NEW PER MONTH

1.
2.
3.

TODAY I'M GRATEFUL FOR

WEDNESDAY
NOVEMBER 2023

15

TODAY'S PRAYER & FOCUS:

SCHEDULE

TIME	APPOINTMENT

PRIORITIES / GOALS

- ○
- ○
- ○
- ○
- ○
- ○
- ○
- ○
- ○
- ○

NOTES & SCRIBBLES

HABITS – 1 NEW PER MONTH

1.
2.
3.

TODAY I'M GRATEFUL FOR

16

THURSDAY
NOVEMBER 2023

TODAY'S PRAYER & FOCUS:

SCHEDULE

TIME	APPOINTMENT

PRIORITIES / GOALS

- ◯
- ◯
- ◯
- ◯
- ◯
- ◯
- ◯
- ◯
- ◯
- ◯

NOTES & SCRIBBLES

HABITS – 1 NEW PER MONTH

1.
2.
3.

TODAY I'M GRATEFUL FOR

FRIDAY
NOVEMBER 2023
17

TODAY'S PRAYER & FOCUS:

SCHEDULE

TIME	APPOINTMENT

PRIORITIES / GOALS

- ○
- ○
- ○
- ○
- ○
- ○
- ○
- ○
- ○
- ○

NOTES & SCRIBBLES

HABITS — 1 NEW PER MONTH

1.
2.
3.

TODAY I'M GRATEFUL FOR

18

SATURDAY
NOVEMBER 2023

TODAY'S PRAYER & FOCUS:

SCHEDULE

TIME	APPOINTMENT

PRIORITIES / GOALS

- ○
- ○
- ○
- ○
- ○
- ○
- ○
- ○
- ○
- ○

NOTES & SCRIBBLES

HABITS – 1 NEW PER MONTH

1.
2.
3.

TODAY I'M GRATEFUL FOR

SUNDAY
NOVEMBER 2023
19

TODAY'S PRAYER & FOCUS:

SCHEDULE

TIME	APPOINTMENT

PRIORITIES / GOALS

- ○
- ○
- ○
- ○
- ○
- ○
- ○
- ○
- ○
- ○

NOTES & SCRIBBLES

HABITS – 1 NEW PER MONTH
1.
2.
3.

TODAY I'M GRATEFUL FOR

WEEKLY PLANNER

QUOTE OF THE WEEK:

MONDAY 20	**PRIORITIES / GOALS**
TUESDAY 21	○ _____
WEDNESDAY 22	○ _____
THURSDAY 23	○ _____
FRIDAY 24	○ _____
SATURDAY 25	**NOTES**
SUNDAY 26	
SUCCESS FOCUS:	

NOVEMBER 20 – 26, 2023

	BREAKFAST	LUNCH	DINNER	SNACKS
M				
T				
W				
T				
F				
S				
S				

SHOPPING LIST:

NOTES

MONDAY
NOVEMBER 2023 **20**

TODAY'S PRAYER & FOCUS:

SCHEDULE

TIME	APPOINTMENT

PRIORITIES / GOALS

- ○
- ○
- ○
- ○
- ○
- ○
- ○
- ○
- ○
- ○

NOTES & SCRIBBLES

HABITS – 1 NEW PER MONTH

1.
2.
3.

TODAY I'M GRATEFUL FOR

21

TUESDAY
NOVEMBER 2023

TODAY'S PRAYER & FOCUS:

SCHEDULE

TIME	APPOINTMENT

PRIORITIES / GOALS

○
○
○
○
○
○
○
○
○
○

NOTES & SCRIBBLES

HABITS – 1 NEW PER MONTH

1.
2.
3.

TODAY I'M GRATEFUL FOR

WEDNESDAY
NOVEMBER 2023 **22**

TODAY'S PRAYER & FOCUS:

SCHEDULE

TIME	APPOINTMENT

PRIORITIES / GOALS

○
○
○
○
○
○
○
○
○
○

NOTES & SCRIBBLES

HABITS – 1 NEW PER MONTH

1.
2.
3.

TODAY I'M GRATEFUL FOR

23 THURSDAY
NOVEMBER 2023

TODAY'S PRAYER & FOCUS:

SCHEDULE

TIME	APPOINTMENT

PRIORITIES / GOALS

- ○
- ○
- ○
- ○
- ○
- ○
- ○
- ○
- ○
- ○

NOTES & SCRIBBLES

HABITS – 1 NEW PER MONTH

1.
2.
3.

TODAY I'M GRATEFUL FOR

FRIDAY
NOVEMBER 2023
24

TODAY'S PRAYER & FOCUS:

SCHEDULE

TIME	APPOINTMENT

PRIORITIES / GOALS

- ◯
- ◯
- ◯
- ◯
- ◯
- ◯
- ◯
- ◯
- ◯
- ◯

NOTES & SCRIBBLES

HABITS – 1 NEW PER MONTH

1.
2.
3.

TODAY I'M GRATEFUL FOR

25
SATURDAY
NOVEMBER 2023

TODAY'S PRAYER & FOCUS:

SCHEDULE

TIME	APPOINTMENT

PRIORITIES / GOALS

- ◯
- ◯
- ◯
- ◯
- ◯
- ◯
- ◯
- ◯
- ◯
- ◯

NOTES & SCRIBBLES

HABITS – 1 NEW PER MONTH

1.
2.
3.

TODAY I'M GRATEFUL FOR

SUNDAY
NOVEMBER 2023
26

TODAY'S PRAYER & FOCUS:

SCHEDULE

TIME	APPOINTMENT

PRIORITIES / GOALS

- ○
- ○
- ○
- ○
- ○
- ○
- ○
- ○
- ○
- ○

NOTES & SCRIBBLES

HABITS – 1 NEW PER MONTH

1.
2.
3.

TODAY I'M GRATEFUL FOR

WEEKLY PLANNER

QUOTE OF THE WEEK:

MONDAY 27	**PRIORITIES / GOALS**
TUESDAY 28	○
WEDNESDAY 29	○
THURSDAY 30	○
FRIDAY 1	○
SATURDAY 2	**NOTES**
SUNDAY 3	

SUCCESS FOCUS:

NOVEMBER 27 – DECEMBER 3, 2023

	BREAKFAST	LUNCH	DINNER	SNACKS
M				
T				
W				
T				
F				
S				
S				

SHOPPING LIST:

NOTES

MONDAY
NOVEMBER 2023 **27**

TODAY'S PRAYER & FOCUS:

SCHEDULE

TIME	APPOINTMENT

PRIORITIES / GOALS

- ○
- ○
- ○
- ○
- ○
- ○
- ○
- ○
- ○
- ○

NOTES & SCRIBBLES

HABITS – 1 NEW PER MONTH

1.
2.
3.

TODAY I'M GRATEFUL FOR

28

TUESDAY
NOVEMBER 2023

TODAY'S PRAYER & FOCUS:

SCHEDULE

TIME	APPOINTMENT

PRIORITIES / GOALS

- ○
- ○
- ○
- ○
- ○
- ○
- ○
- ○
- ○
- ○

NOTES & SCRIBBLES

HABITS – 1 NEW PER MONTH

1.
2.
3.

TODAY I'M GRATEFUL FOR

WEDNESDAY
NOVEMBER 2023 — 29

TODAY'S PRAYER & FOCUS:

SCHEDULE

TIME	APPOINTMENT

PRIORITIES / GOALS

- ◯
- ◯
- ◯
- ◯
- ◯
- ◯
- ◯
- ◯
- ◯
- ◯

NOTES & SCRIBBLES

HABITS – 1 NEW PER MONTH

1.
2.
3.

TODAY I'M GRATEFUL FOR

30
THURSDAY
NOVEMBER 2023

TODAY'S PRAYER & FOCUS:

SCHEDULE

TIME	APPOINTMENT

PRIORITIES / GOALS

- ○
- ○
- ○
- ○
- ○
- ○
- ○
- ○
- ○
- ○

NOTES & SCRIBBLES

HABITS – 1 NEW PER MONTH

1.
2.
3.

TODAY I'M GRATEFUL FOR

FRIDAY
DECEMBER 2023

1

TODAY'S PRAYER & FOCUS:

SCHEDULE

TIME	APPOINTMENT

PRIORITIES / GOALS

- ○
- ○
- ○
- ○
- ○
- ○
- ○
- ○
- ○
- ○

NOTES & SCRIBBLES

HABITS – 1 NEW PER MONTH

1.
2.
3.

TODAY I'M GRATEFUL FOR

2

SATURDAY
DECEMBER 2023

TODAY'S PRAYER & FOCUS:

SCHEDULE

TIME	APPOINTMENT

PRIORITIES / GOALS

- ○
- ○
- ○
- ○
- ○
- ○
- ○
- ○
- ○
- ○

NOTES & SCRIBBLES

HABITS – 1 NEW PER MONTH

1.
2.
3.

TODAY I'M GRATEFUL FOR

SUNDAY
DECEMBER 2023

3

TODAY'S PRAYER & FOCUS:

SCHEDULE

TIME	APPOINTMENT

PRIORITIES / GOALS

- ◯
- ◯
- ◯
- ◯
- ◯
- ◯
- ◯
- ◯
- ◯
- ◯

NOTES & SCRIBBLES

HABITS – 1 NEW PER MONTH

1.
2.
3.

TODAY I'M GRATEFUL FOR

NOVEMBER 2023 INCOME TRACKER

DATE	INCOME	CATEGORY	AMOUNT
TOTAL			

NOVEMBER 2023 EXPENSE TRACKER

DATE	EXPENSE	CATEGORY	AMOUNT
TOTAL			

NOVEMBER 2023 SAVINGS TRACKER

SAVING FOR: _____   GOAL AMOUNT: _____

DATE	NOTES	AMOUNT	BALANCE
TOTAL			

MONTHLY PROGRESS - NOVEMBER 2023

I HAVE ACHIEVED...

I AM THANKFUL...

I'D LIKE TO IMPROVE...

HOW I WILL CELEBRATE WHAT I DID WELL...

DECEMBER

MONDAY	TUESDAY	WEDNESDAY	THURSDAY
4	5	6	7
11	12	13	14
18	19	20	21
25	26	27	28

GOALS

2023

FRIDAY	SATURDAY	SUNDAY	NOTES
1	2	3	
8	9	10	
15	16	17	
22	23	24	
29	30	31	

NOTES

MASTER SUCCESS ACTIONS
DECEMBER 2023

List 4 life areas and your goals to focus on this month:

1.

2.

3.

4.

Use this master task list for the big action steps you will commit to do this month. They will accomplish the goals you set to improve your life in the 4 areas of focus. Your daily tasks will be the small steps to accomplish these bigger steps.

DONE	SUCCESS ACTIONS

NOTES

WEEKLY PLANNER

QUOTE OF THE WEEK:

MONDAY 4
TUESDAY 5
WEDNESDAY 6
THURSDAY 7
FRIDAY 8
SATURDAY 9
SUNDAY 10

SUCCESS FOCUS:

PRIORITIES / GOALS

○
○
○
○
○
○
○
○
○
○

NOTES

DECEMBER 4 – 10, 2023

	BREAKFAST	LUNCH	DINNER	SNACKS
M				
T				
W				
T				
F				
S				
S				

SHOPPING LIST:

NOTES

MONDAY
DECEMBER 2023

4

TODAY'S PRAYER & FOCUS:

SCHEDULE

TIME	APPOINTMENT

PRIORITIES / GOALS

- ○
- ○
- ○
- ○
- ○
- ○
- ○
- ○
- ○
- ○

NOTES & SCRIBBLES

HABITS – 1 NEW PER MONTH

1.
2.
3.

TODAY I'M GRATEFUL FOR

5

TUESDAY
DECEMBER 2023

TODAY'S PRAYER & FOCUS:

SCHEDULE

TIME	APPOINTMENT

PRIORITIES / GOALS

- ◯
- ◯
- ◯
- ◯
- ◯
- ◯
- ◯
- ◯
- ◯
- ◯

NOTES & SCRIBBLES

HABITS – 1 NEW PER MONTH

1.
2.
3.

TODAY I'M GRATEFUL FOR

WEDNESDAY
DECEMBER 2023

6

TODAY'S PRAYER & FOCUS:

SCHEDULE

TIME	APPOINTMENT

PRIORITIES / GOALS

- ○
- ○
- ○
- ○
- ○
- ○
- ○
- ○
- ○
- ○

NOTES & SCRIBBLES

HABITS – 1 NEW PER MONTH

1.
2.
3.

TODAY I'M GRATEFUL FOR

7

THURSDAY
DECEMBER 2023

TODAY'S PRAYER & FOCUS:

SCHEDULE

TIME	APPOINTMENT

PRIORITIES / GOALS

- ○
- ○
- ○
- ○
- ○
- ○
- ○
- ○
- ○
- ○

NOTES & SCRIBBLES

HABITS – 1 NEW PER MONTH

1.
2.
3.

TODAY I'M GRATEFUL FOR

FRIDAY
DECEMBER 2023
8

TODAY'S PRAYER & FOCUS:

SCHEDULE

TIME	APPOINTMENT

PRIORITIES / GOALS

- ○
- ○
- ○
- ○
- ○
- ○
- ○
- ○
- ○
- ○

NOTES & SCRIBBLES

HABITS – 1 NEW PER MONTH

1.
2.
3.

TODAY I'M GRATEFUL FOR

9

SATURDAY
DECEMBER 2023

TODAY'S PRAYER & FOCUS:

SCHEDULE

TIME	APPOINTMENT

PRIORITIES / GOALS

- ○
- ○
- ○
- ○
- ○
- ○
- ○
- ○
- ○
- ○

NOTES & SCRIBBLES

HABITS – 1 NEW PER MONTH

1.
2.
3.

TODAY I'M GRATEFUL FOR

SUNDAY
DECEMBER 2023
10

TODAY'S PRAYER & FOCUS:

SCHEDULE

TIME	APPOINTMENT

PRIORITIES / GOALS

- ○
- ○
- ○
- ○
- ○
- ○
- ○
- ○
- ○
- ○

NOTES & SCRIBBLES

HABITS – 1 NEW PER MONTH

1.
2.
3.

TODAY I'M GRATEFUL FOR

WEEKLY PLANNER

QUOTE OF THE WEEK:

MONDAY 11
TUESDAY 12
WEDNESDAY 13
THURSDAY 14
FRIDAY 15
SATURDAY 16
SUNDAY 17

SUCCESS FOCUS:

PRIORITIES / GOALS

○ ....
○ ....
○ ....
○ ....
○ ....
○ ....
○ ....
○ ....
○ ....

NOTES

DECEMBER 11 – 17, 2023

	BREAKFAST	LUNCH	DINNER	SNACKS
M				
T				
W				
T				
F				
S				
S				

SHOPPING LIST:

NOTES

MONDAY
DECEMBER 2023
11

TODAY'S PRAYER & FOCUS:

SCHEDULE

TIME	APPOINTMENT

PRIORITIES / GOALS

- ◯
- ◯
- ◯
- ◯
- ◯
- ◯
- ◯
- ◯
- ◯
- ◯

NOTES & SCRIBBLES

HABITS – 1 NEW PER MONTH

1.
2.
3.

TODAY I'M GRATEFUL FOR

12

TUESDAY
DECEMBER 2023

TODAY'S PRAYER & FOCUS:

SCHEDULE

TIME	APPOINTMENT

PRIORITIES / GOALS

○
○
○
○
○
○
○
○
○
○

NOTES & SCRIBBLES

HABITS — 1 NEW PER MONTH

1.
2.
3.

TODAY I'M GRATEFUL FOR

WEDNESDAY
DECEMBER 2023
13

TODAY'S PRAYER & FOCUS:

SCHEDULE

TIME	APPOINTMENT

PRIORITIES / GOALS

- ◯
- ◯
- ◯
- ◯
- ◯
- ◯
- ◯
- ◯
- ◯
- ◯

NOTES & SCRIBBLES

HABITS – 1 NEW PER MONTH

1.
2.
3.

TODAY I'M GRATEFUL FOR

14

THURSDAY
DECEMBER 2023

TODAY'S PRAYER & FOCUS:

SCHEDULE

TIME	APPOINTMENT

PRIORITIES / GOALS

- ○
- ○
- ○
- ○
- ○
- ○
- ○
- ○
- ○
- ○

NOTES & SCRIBBLES

HABITS – 1 NEW PER MONTH

1.
2.
3.

TODAY I'M GRATEFUL FOR

FRIDAY
DECEMBER 2023
15

TODAY'S PRAYER & FOCUS:

SCHEDULE

TIME	APPOINTMENT

PRIORITIES / GOALS

- ○
- ○
- ○
- ○
- ○
- ○
- ○
- ○
- ○
- ○

NOTES & SCRIBBLES

HABITS – 1 NEW PER MONTH

1.
2.
3.

TODAY I'M GRATEFUL FOR

16

SATURDAY
DECEMBER 2023

TODAY'S PRAYER & FOCUS:

SCHEDULE

TIME	APPOINTMENT

PRIORITIES / GOALS

- ○
- ○
- ○
- ○
- ○
- ○
- ○
- ○
- ○
- ○

NOTES & SCRIBBLES

HABITS — 1 NEW PER MONTH

1.
2.
3.

TODAY I'M GRATEFUL FOR

SUNDAY
DECEMBER 2023
17

TODAY'S PRAYER & FOCUS:

SCHEDULE

TIME	APPOINTMENT

PRIORITIES / GOALS

- ○
- ○
- ○
- ○
- ○
- ○
- ○
- ○
- ○
- ○

NOTES & SCRIBBLES

HABITS — 1 NEW PER MONTH

1.
2.
3.

TODAY I'M GRATEFUL FOR

WEEKLY PLANNER

QUOTE OF THE WEEK:

MONDAY 18	
TUESDAY 19	
WEDNESDAY 20	
THURSDAY 21	
FRIDAY 22	
SATURDAY 23	
SUNDAY 24	

SUCCESS FOCUS:

PRIORITIES / GOALS

○
○
○
○
○
○
○
○
○
○

NOTES

DECEMBER 18 – 24, 2023

	BREAKFAST	LUNCH	DINNER	SNACKS
M				
T				
W				
T				
F				
S				
S				

SHOPPING LIST:

NOTES

MONDAY
DECEMBER 2023
18

TODAY'S PRAYER & FOCUS:

SCHEDULE

TIME	APPOINTMENT

PRIORITIES / GOALS

- ○
- ○
- ○
- ○
- ○
- ○
- ○
- ○
- ○
- ○

NOTES & SCRIBBLES

HABITS – 1 NEW PER MONTH

1.
2.
3.

TODAY I'M GRATEFUL FOR

19

TUESDAY
DECEMBER 2023

TODAY'S PRAYER & FOCUS:

SCHEDULE

TIME	APPOINTMENT

PRIORITIES / GOALS

- ○
- ○
- ○
- ○
- ○
- ○
- ○
- ○
- ○
- ○

NOTES & SCRIBBLES

HABITS – 1 NEW PER MONTH

1.
2.
3.

TODAY I'M GRATEFUL FOR

WEDNESDAY
DECEMBER 2023   **20**

TODAY'S PRAYER & FOCUS:

SCHEDULE

TIME	APPOINTMENT

PRIORITIES / GOALS

- ○
- ○
- ○
- ○
- ○
- ○
- ○
- ○
- ○
- ○

NOTES & SCRIBBLES

HABITS – 1 NEW PER MONTH

1.
2.
3.

TODAY I'M GRATEFUL FOR

21

THURSDAY
DECEMBER 2023

TODAY'S PRAYER & FOCUS:

SCHEDULE

TIME	APPOINTMENT

PRIORITIES / GOALS

- ◯
- ◯
- ◯
- ◯
- ◯
- ◯
- ◯
- ◯
- ◯
- ◯

NOTES & SCRIBBLES

HABITS – 1 NEW PER MONTH

1.
2.
3.

TODAY I'M GRATEFUL FOR

FRIDAY
DECEMBER 2023
22

TODAY'S PRAYER & FOCUS:

SCHEDULE

TIME	APPOINTMENT

PRIORITIES / GOALS

○
○
○
○
○
○
○
○
○
○

NOTES & SCRIBBLES

HABITS – 1 NEW PER MONTH

1.
2.
3.

TODAY I'M GRATEFUL FOR

23

SATURDAY
DECEMBER 2023

TODAY'S PRAYER & FOCUS:

SCHEDULE

TIME	APPOINTMENT

PRIORITIES / GOALS

- ◯
- ◯
- ◯
- ◯
- ◯
- ◯
- ◯
- ◯
- ◯
- ◯

NOTES & SCRIBBLES

HABITS – 1 NEW PER MONTH

1.
2.
3.

TODAY I'M GRATEFUL FOR

SUNDAY
DECEMBER 2023
24

TODAY'S PRAYER & FOCUS:

SCHEDULE

TIME	APPOINTMENT

PRIORITIES / GOALS

- ◯
- ◯
- ◯
- ◯
- ◯
- ◯
- ◯
- ◯
- ◯
- ◯

NOTES & SCRIBBLES

HABITS – 1 NEW PER MONTH

1.
2.
3.

TODAY I'M GRATEFUL FOR

WEEKLY PLANNER

QUOTE OF THE WEEK:

MONDAY 25
TUESDAY 26
WEDNESDAY 27
THURSDAY 28
FRIDAY 29
SATURDAY 30
SUNDAY 31

SUCCESS FOCUS:

PRIORITIES / GOALS

○
○
○
○
○
○
○
○
○
○

NOTES

DECEMBER 25 – 31, 2023

	BREAKFAST	LUNCH	DINNER	SNACKS
M				
T				
W				
T				
F				
S				
S				

SHOPPING LIST:

NOTES

MONDAY
DECEMBER 2023
25

TODAY'S PRAYER & FOCUS:

SCHEDULE

TIME	APPOINTMENT

PRIORITIES / GOALS

- ◯
- ◯
- ◯
- ◯
- ◯
- ◯
- ◯
- ◯
- ◯
- ◯

NOTES & SCRIBBLES

HABITS – 1 NEW PER MONTH

1.
2.
3.

TODAY I'M GRATEFUL FOR

26

TUESDAY
DECEMBER 2023

TODAY'S PRAYER & FOCUS:

SCHEDULE

TIME	APPOINTMENT

PRIORITIES / GOALS

- ○
- ○
- ○
- ○
- ○
- ○
- ○
- ○
- ○
- ○

NOTES & SCRIBBLES

HABITS – 1 NEW PER MONTH

1.
2.
3.

TODAY I'M GRATEFUL FOR

WEDNESDAY
DECEMBER 2023
27

TODAY'S PRAYER & FOCUS:

SCHEDULE

TIME	APPOINTMENT

PRIORITIES / GOALS

- ○
- ○
- ○
- ○
- ○
- ○
- ○
- ○
- ○
- ○

NOTES & SCRIBBLES

HABITS – 1 NEW PER MONTH
1.
2.
3.

TODAY I'M GRATEFUL FOR

28

THURSDAY
DECEMBER 2023

TODAY'S PRAYER & FOCUS:

SCHEDULE

TIME	APPOINTMENT

PRIORITIES / GOALS

- ○
- ○
- ○
- ○
- ○
- ○
- ○
- ○
- ○
- ○

NOTES & SCRIBBLES

HABITS – 1 NEW PER MONTH

1.
2.
3.

TODAY I'M GRATEFUL FOR

FRIDAY **29**
DECEMBER 2023

TODAY'S PRAYER & FOCUS:

SCHEDULE

TIME	APPOINTMENT

PRIORITIES / GOALS

- ○
- ○
- ○
- ○
- ○
- ○
- ○
- ○
- ○
- ○

NOTES & SCRIBBLES

HABITS – 1 NEW PER MONTH

1.
2.
3.

TODAY I'M GRATEFUL FOR

30 SATURDAY
DECEMBER 2023

TODAY'S PRAYER & FOCUS:

SCHEDULE

TIME	APPOINTMENT

PRIORITIES / GOALS

- ○
- ○
- ○
- ○
- ○
- ○
- ○
- ○
- ○

NOTES & SCRIBBLES

HABITS — 1 NEW PER MONTH

1.
2.
3.

TODAY I'M GRATEFUL FOR

SUNDAY
DECEMBER 2023
31

TODAY'S PRAYER & FOCUS:

SCHEDULE

TIME	APPOINTMENT

PRIORITIES / GOALS

- ○
- ○
- ○
- ○
- ○
- ○
- ○
- ○
- ○
- ○

NOTES & SCRIBBLES

HABITS – 1 NEW PER MONTH

1.
2.
3.

TODAY I'M GRATEFUL FOR

DECEMBER 2023 INCOME TRACKER

DATE	INCOME	CATEGORY	AMOUNT
TOTAL			

DECEMBER 2023 EXPENSE TRACKER

DATE	EXPENSE	CATEGORY	AMOUNT
TOTAL			

DECEMBER 2023 SAVINGS TRACKER

SAVING FOR: _____ GOAL AMOUNT: _____

DATE	NOTES	AMOUNT	BALANCE
TOTAL			

MONTHLY PROGRESS - DECEMBER 2023

I HAVE ACHIEVED...

I AM THANKFUL...

I'D LIKE TO IMPROVE...

HOW I WILL CELEBRATE WHAT I DID WELL...

BOOKS TO READ

TITLE	AUTHOR	✓

WISH LIST

PRODUCT	PRICE	STORE

NOTES

NOTES

NOTES

NOTES

NOTES

NOTES

NOTES

NOTES

NOTES

NOTES

NOTES

NOTES

NOTES

NOTES

NOTES

NOTES

NOTES

NOTES

NOTES

NOTES

INDEX

TOPIC	PAGE(S)

INDEX

TOPIC	PAGE(S)

INDEX

TOPIC	PAGE(S)

INDEX

TOPIC	PAGE(S)

www.ingramcontent.com/pod-product-compliance
Lightning Source LLC
Chambersburg PA
CBHW071742150426
43191CB00010B/1662